Time Management For Kids

A. T. Sorsa

Book Cover by the author

Illustrations by the author

This is combined version of Time Management for Boys and Time Management for Girls – books

2nd edition 2024

Contents

Foreword

Welcome to Time Management For Kids. This is a quick help book.

As a child, learning to manage your time effectively is one of the most powerful skills you can develop. It's the key to achieving your goals, reducing stress, and unlocking a sense of pride and accomplishment that will stay with you for the rest of your life. In today's fast-paced world, kids are juggling more responsibilities than ever before – from schoolwork and extracurricular activities to friendships and family commitments. It's easy to feel overwhelmed and unsure of where to start. That's why this book is so important. Within these pages, you'll discover practical tips, fun strategies, and inspiring stories to help you prioritize, organize, and make the most of your time.

You'll learn how to:

- Set achievable goals and create a schedule that works for you

- Prioritize tasks and avoid procrastination

- Balance schoolwork, playtime, and rest

- Use technology wisely and avoid distractions

- Build healthy habits and self-care routines

Most importantly, you'll discover that time management isn't about being perfect - it's about being intentional, flexible, and kind to yourself. As you embark on this journey, remember that every small step counts. You have the power to take control of your time and create a life that truly reflects your values, passions, and dreams.

This book is written in form of lists. It's fast to read and use as a reminder what you can do to be organized and manage your time.

It also includes a short story of Timmy and the Time Machine.

So, if you are ready, let's get started!

Chapter One

Time does not play favorites

EVERYONE HAS THE SAME 24-hour day to do our chores and tasks. It is just 1,440 minutes for all the daily tasks. It's not so much when you have homework and other chores to do, and you want to play, too.

Time flies!

Time is ticking!

Do you know how many hours are in a day? Not as many as you think! When you waste time or put things off until later, the hours start to disappear. You spend some hours at school, learning and having fun with friends. But after school, your time is limited. You have just enough time to:

- Do your homework

- Study for tests

- Play outside

- Read a book

- Play a game

- Watch television or

- Pursue your favorite hobbies!

So, let's make a plan! Let's use our time wisely and make the most of every hour. What will you do with your time today?

STUDY AND PLAY TIME

Chapter Two

Plan What You Do

BE THE BOSS OF Your Time!

Do you want to feel happy and proud of how you spend your day?

Start by making a plan!

When you plan ahead:

- You'll know exactly what to do and when to do it.

- You'll feel proud of all you accomplish.

- You'll have time for fun and play.

Time to Change Your Habits!

Want to be better at using your time?

Try these simple steps:

- Pay attention to what you do each day.

- Make a list of what needs to be done to-day, tomorrow, and this week.

- Choose the best time for each task.

It's Easy as 1-2-3!

Write down what you need to do.

Check your schedule and choose a time.

Do it!

You're in Charge!

By planning and paying attention, you'll be amazed at how much you can do!

Chapter Three

Sleep Time

Sleepy Time is Important!

Do you want to be bright-eyed and bushy-tailed for school tomorrow?

You need sleep!

Sleep is like a magic recharge for your body. It

- Makes you feel fresh and new

- Helps your body heal and grow strong

- Gets you ready for another fun day!

SLEEP TIME

How Much Sleep Do You Need?

Most kids need at least 8 hours of sleep each night.

Some might need more; some might need less.

But here's the important part:

You need uninterrupted sleep!

That means:

- No waking up in the middle of the night

- No TV or screens before bed

- A cozy, quiet bedroom all to yourself!

Sleep Tight!

When you get good sleep:

- You'll wake up feeling happy and re-freshed

- You'll be ready to learn and play

- You'll tackle challenges with a big smile!

What Happens When You Don't Get Enough Sleep?

Uh-oh! If you don't get enough sleep:

- You'll feel sleepy and tired all day

- You'll yawn and rub your eyes to stay awake

But it won't work!

- **Tired Brain = Tired Body**

When you're tired:

- You can't focus or pay attention

- You can't learn new things easily

- Your brain gets a little mixed up!

Imagine Trying to:

- Do a math test with sleepy eyes

- Read a book with a foggy brain

- Play outside with heavy legs

It's Hard to Do Your Best!

But don't worry! When you get enough sleep:

- Your brain is sharp and clear

- Your body is strong and energetic

Chapter Four

What is Time Management?

Do you want to get more done in less time?

Time management is the secret!

What is Time Management?

Time management is a superpower that helps you:

- Set goals and objectives

- Make to-do lists

- Break tasks into smaller steps

- Prioritize what's important

- Be the Boss of Your Time!

With time management skills, you'll learn to:

- Control your actions and tasks

- Make good choices

- Get more done in less time!

Plan Ahead, Succeed Ahead!

When you plan and manage your time:

- You'll finish tasks on time

- You'll reach your goals

- You'll feel happy and confident!

Time Management Superstars!

Have you ever noticed that some people get a lot done and seem to have plenty of time?

What's Their Secret?

Maybe they were born with great planning skills, or maybe they learned how to:

- Use their time wisely

- Plan ahead

- Stay focused

The Magic Word: Discipline

These time management superstars know that:

- Wasting time doesn't lead to success

- Hard work and effort pay off

- Staying on track is key!

Anyone Can Learn!

You can become a time management superstar too!

By practicing:

- Goal-setting

- Prioritizing

- Staying organized

You Can Do It!

Remember: Success comes from hard work and effort!

Good time management skills can be learned.

You have the power to achieve your goals!

Chapter Five

Why Time management?

Why Learn Time Management?

- To achieve more in less time

- To improve your performance

- To feel proud of what you accomplish!

Why Organize?

Do you want to achieve your dreams and goals?

Organizing and managing your time is the key!

Here's Why and what happens when you are organized:

- Get better grades at school

- Finish tasks and chores on time

- Excel in sports and activities

- Learn new skills and hobbies

Be Your Best Self!

When you organize and prioritize:
- You develop self-discipline

- You become a better student

- You excel in other areas of life

- You'll be ready for future success!

Dream Big!

What do you want to achieve?

- Be a star cheerleader?

- Be a star player?

- Swim to victory?

- Shine as a ballet dancer?

- Create amazing art?

- Write a bestseller?

- Shine on stage?

Make Your Dreams Happen!

By learning time management and organization skills:

- You'll reach your goals faster

- You'll feel proud of yourself

- You'll unlock your full potential!

Imagine Your Dream Day!

Picture yourself doing all the things you love:

- Playing soccer with friends?

- Painting a masterpiece?

- Reading a favorite book?

- Riding your bike?

But Where's the Time?

To do all these awesome things, you need time!

The Secret to More Time: **Time Management!**

To get more time for fun:

- Organize your tasks

- Prioritize what's important

- Manage your time wisely

- Make Time for Fun!

When you use time management skills:

- You'll have more time for hobbies

- You'll enjoy your favorite activities

- You'll make your dreams happen!

Take Control of Your Time!

Remember:

Time management is the key to doing what you love and making your dreams come true!

Anything you want requires time.

Wishing Won't Make It Happen! Do you want better grades at school? Don't just wish upon a star!

No Magic Solutions!

- The tooth fairy won't leave good grades under your pillow

- The Sandman won't bring test answers in your dreams

- Twinkling stars won't grant better grades

- Santa Claus won't leave an A+ report card under the tree

You Hold the Power!

To get better grades:

- Study hard every day

- Listen in class and take notes

- Ask questions and seek help

- Practice and review regularly

Your Effort = Better Grades!

Remember: Wishing is not enough!

Hard work and effort lead to success!

The Secret to Success!

Want better grades? It takes:

- Hard work

- Discipline

- Self-control

What Does Self-Discipline Mean at school?

It means:

- Listening to your teacher

- Taking notes

- Finishing homework and projects

- Understanding what you're doing

- Preparing for the next day

Doing What's Necessary

Sometimes you'll do things you don't love...To achieve your dreams!

Unlock Your Potential!

Self-discipline, time management, organization, and prioritization will help you:

- Get better grades

- Become a better athlete

- Excel in art or music

- Reach your dreams!

You Got This!

Remember:

Discipline today = Success tomorrow

Hard work pays off!

Chapter Six

Time Management Through the Ages!

Did you know that time management has changed over time?

Your Great-Grandparents' Way

They used:

- Paper notes to remind themselves

- Sticky notes on the fridge

- Calendars on the wall

They also used appointment notebooks to write down their meetings and tasks. These notebooks and watches helped to set daily and weekly goals. You can also use these if you like.

Your Grandparents' Method

They relied on:

- Clocks and watches to stay on track

- Paper planners and agendas

- Wall calendars and desktop calendars

- Memory and routine

Your Parents' Approach

They use:

- Digital calendars on phones and computers

- Reminders on their devices

- Apps to stay organized

They also used appointment notebooks to write down their meetings and tasks. These notebooks and watches helped to set daily and weekly goals.

You will hear your parents talking about cell phone reminders to do something at a specific day or time.

Digital Helpers!

Do you know how your parents and older siblings stay organized?

They use:

- Planner and calendar apps

- On their computers, phones, and laptops

To keep track of daily tasks.

These digital helpers:

- Remind them of important tasks

- Help prioritize what's important

- Set daily and weekly goals

- Keep track of schedules

And Now, Your Turn!

Stay on Track!

With digital planners:

You can:

- See what needs to be done

- Make a plan to get it done

- Reach your goals

Digital Tools for You!

You can use:

- Digital calendars

- Task lists

- Reminders

- Goal-setting apps

Get Organized, Stay Happy!

Chapter Seven

The Boy Who Invented a Time Machine

TIMMY WAS A BRIGHT and curious 9-year-old, but he had one major problem: time management.

Timmy had trouble getting his chores done in time. He forgot to do his homework at least once a week and got F-grades because he never returned his homework to his teacher.

Every morning, he was late. Timmy was always the last one running after the bus or panting inside the bus after running from home to the bus stop.

Many mornings he missed the bus and had to go back and ask his parents, "Hey, I missed the bus again. Can one of you take me to school this morning?"

His parents were at their wit's end. "Not again, Timmy!" they'd sigh, shaking their heads.

But he was desperate. He just could not understand what was wrong with him. He started doing his chores, but then he saw an interesting television show, or his friend called, or he started playing with his basketball in the backyard and forgot to do his chores. The time flew and Timmy had again used all his spare time playing, chatting with his friends and watching television. And then it was time to go to bed.

Timmy was determined to change. One weekend, he decided to take matters into his own hands. He rummaged through the garage and gathered scrap metal, an old sofa, tools, a hairdryer, a TV, a toaster, and duct tape.

It took Timmy all day to finish his time machine –project.

He was exhausted after a long day of work, but he was very proud of the new time machine when it was ready. Timmy was only nine years old and had already built a time machine. He was a genius!

He thought that when everybody would hear about his successful invention, he would earn millions of dollars, and maybe he would not have to go to school after that.

He decided that he would give some of his money to his parents so they would not have to work either. He was not so sure if he would give any money tohis older brother because he always teased him, like that one time when he had put spiders in his bed, or glue in his socks, or when he had taken off the screws from the door hinges and the door fell in when Timmy tried to open it.

Timmy was sure that after inventing a time machine he would not have to go to school or to work. Maybe he would have to go to school to learn the maintenance of the time machine, and how to invest his money. But otherwise, why would he have to go to school if he was already rich and famous inventor?!

This is what Timmy's time machine looked like:

He decided to try his machine right away. He set all the three clocks to a different time, and then he sat inside on the old couch and turned the knobs and pulled the steering sticks. He was ready to go back in time to the previous Monday when he had not returned his homework.

He waited and waited.

Nothing happened.

Then Timmy had an idea: *What if the time has changed?* He thought *I just don't know it because I'm in the time machine! I better go and check from my mom what time it is now!*

"Mom! What day it is?" Timmy shouted when he ran inside.

"Timmy, you should know that it is Saturday because you are not at school today. It's your day off," Timmy's mother answered.

He was so disappointed. He had believed his machine would work, and he would be able to fix his homework by travelling back intime. Now he realized that if he wanted to do his homework and return them intime, he would have to concentrate and not be distracted. He would have to learn to set up the alarm clock in the morning in order to wake up on time. He would have to leave his home on time in order to be on time for the bus. There were no shortcuts. It was all up to him. Nobody else could make him be in time and be organized.

After that weekend, Timmy was never late from school, never missed his school bus, and never forgot to return his homework on time.

This is how he succeeded in his time management project: Timmy used task lists and prioritized his tasks. He also used highlighters, sticky notes and colorful flags to mark important parts in the books he read.

Then he tried the weekly and monthly planners, which made his time management even easier.

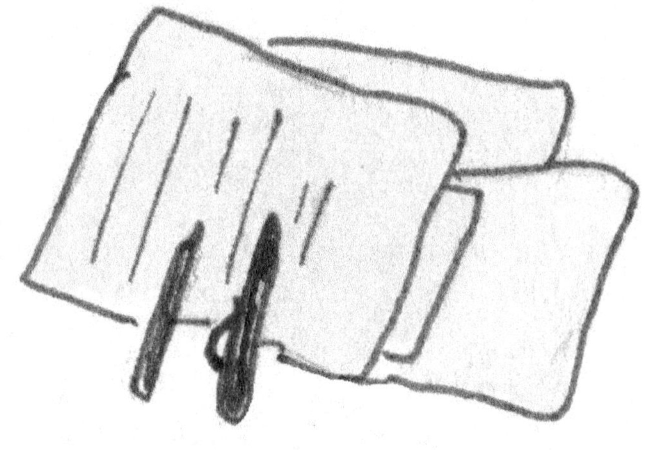

Timmy made lots of notes. He also had two alarm clocks so he would not miss going to school on time and would not miss his bus.

He had a folder for all his homework and other school papers to put in his backpack.

He arranged his folder according to the subject:
Math papers to Math-folder, Earth Science -papers to Earth Science– folder, and so on.

He had notebooks and extra pencils for school.

By using his folder, Timmy was able to keep his backpack organized and neat. He had a pencil case for his pencils and erasers so that they would not get lost in his backpack.

This is what Timmy's backpack looked like:

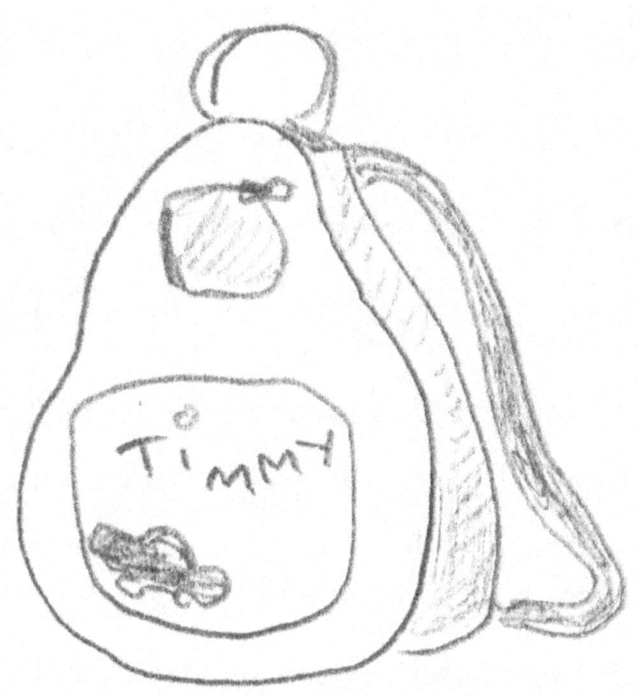

Timmy's Planning Upgrade

Timmy's big wall calendar helped him see the whole month, plan ahead, and stay on track with home tasks. But he soon realized it wasn't enough.

I need something more, Timmy thought.

The problem? He'd forget to mark important tasks and deadlines on his wall calendar.

Solution?

A small planner!

Now Timmy could carry his planner everywhere, jotting down crucial dates during the school day. He added colorful flags to highlight urgent tasks and deadlines.

To ensure seamless transitions between school and home, Timmy wrote sticky notes in his planner. When he got home, he'd transfer the notes to his wall calendar.

Timmy's Planning System:

- Big wall calendar (home)

- Small planner (school)

- Colorful flags (deadlines)

- Sticky notes (transferable reminders)

With this dynamic duo, Timmy stayed organized and on top of tasks:

- No more forgotten deadlines

- No more missed tasks

- Smooth transitions between school and home

Timmy's planning system was complete! His wall calendar looked like this:

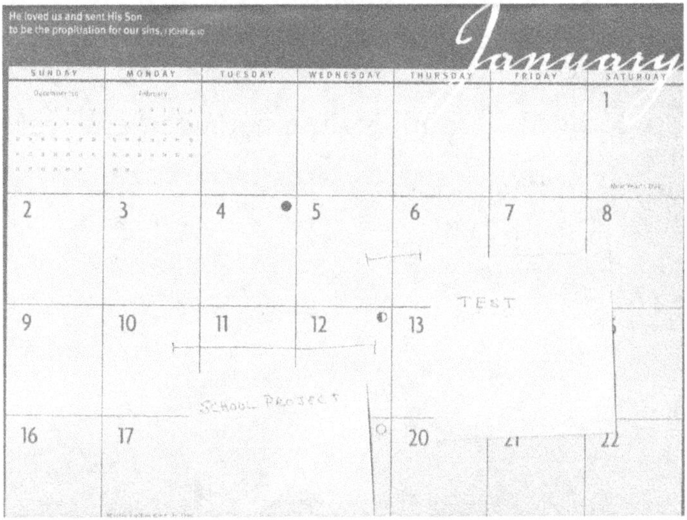

This is how Timmy's planner looked like:

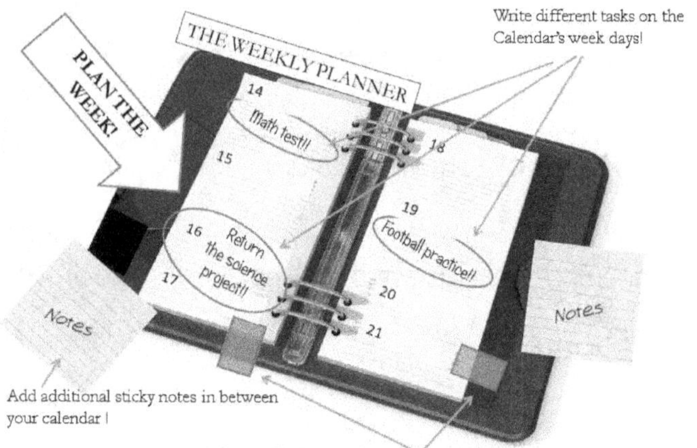

The next pages will show you how he finally managed to get organized. They will tell you more about Timmie's time management techniques and methods.

Chapter Eight

Mastering Time Management for Learning

EFFECTIVE TIME MANAGEMENT BOOSTS your productivity while reading, doing homework, and studying.

Go Beyond Homework: Learning is more than just completing assignments. To truly understand and retain information:

Summarize

- Write your own summary of what you've read

- Note key characters, plot, and main ideas

- Review your notes for quick recall

Take Notes

- Record important points while reading

- Review notes to answer questions and recall key concepts

Sticky Notes and Flags

- Mark important pages with colored flags

- Write key points, conclusions, or reminders on sticky notes

- Place sticky notes in strategic spots for quick reminders

Sticky Notes to the Rescue!

- Need to remember something for tomorrow?

- Write a sticky note and place it where you'll see it

Time Management Tips:

1. Summarize what you read

2. Take notes while reading

3. Use sticky notes and flags for quick review

4. Review notes regularly

By following these tips, you'll:

- Save time

- Improve retention

- Boost productivity

Color Your Way to Success!

Flagging System

Use colorful flags to categorize information:

- Red: Most important

- Yellow: Interesting to know

- Blue: Key topic

- Create your own color code!

- Write topics on flags

- Use different flag sizes

- Personalize your study routine and style

Make Learning Fun!

- Add color to your school day

- Use flags, sticky notes, and highlighters

- Make studying engaging and enjoyable

Track Your Progress

- Follow your color coding and notes

- Watch your time management improve

- Celebrate your success!

The Power of Highlighters

- Save time

- Focus on key information

- Learn faster

Why Highlighters Matter:

- Highlight important text

- Review quickly

- Learn efficiently

- Repeat and retain information

Time Management Tip: *Highlighting = Time Saved*

- Less time reviewing

- More time for learning

- Better retention

Collaborate and Highlight!

School Projects Made Easy

Working with classmates? Highlight essential topic points to:

- Ensure key coverage

- Focus on crucial information

Highlighter Options Galore! Choose your favorite:

- Thin to thick highlighters

- Pen-highlighter combos

- Erasable highlighters

- Highlighters with flags

Highlight Smart, Not Hard! Avoid over-highlighting:

- Too much color = messy pages

- Goal: Easy reference, not rainbow chaos!

Highlighting Tips:

- Focus on key phrases

- Use colors strategically

- Review and adjust

Stay on Track with Calendars! Keep tabs on:

* Projects

* Homework

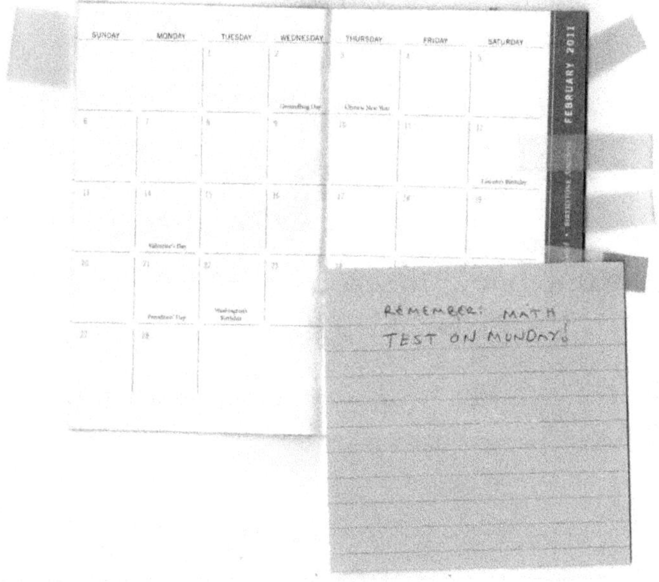

Keep extra pencils, pens and erasers with you just in case you lose or misplace one.

Use **notebooks** for extra notes!

Chapter Nine

What is a Task List?

What is a Task List?

A task list is a simple yet powerful tool!

Your Daily To-Do List

- Map out tasks to complete

- Inventory of chores for the day

- Helps you remember, divide, and prioritize tasks

How Task Lists Work

Just like a grocery store manager tracks inventory, you track tasks:

* Know what needs to be done

* Focus on essential tasks

* Achieve goals efficiently

Task List Benefits

* Improves memory

* Breaks tasks into manageable chunks

* Prioritizes urgent tasks

* Enhances productivity

* Reduces stress

Create Your Task List Today!

Write down:

* Daily chores

* Short-term goals

* Long-term objectives

* Deadlines

Review, Revise, Repeat!

Regularly update your list to stay on track.

A
B
C
D
X

Multiple Lists or One?

Choose what works best for you:

- One comprehensive list

- Multiple lists for different tasks or categories

Benefits of Multiple Lists

- Divide tasks by priority or category

- Easier time management

- Improved organization

Prioritize with Letter Lists

Consider using:

- A-List: Urgent and high-priority tasks

- B-List: Important but less urgent tasks

- C-List: Medium-priority tasks

- D-List: Low-priority tasks

- X-List: Tasks to delegate or eliminate

Track Progress

When completing a task:

- Cross it off your list

- Feel accomplished and motivated

Tips:

- Review and adjust lists regularly

- Keep lists concise and manageable

- Use colors or symbols for visual organization

Find a style that works for YOU!

When you are done,

Check It Off!

DONE!

Celebrate Your Progress!

Crossing off or checking completed tasks:

- Tracks progress

- Shows accomplishments

- Boosts satisfaction and motivation

- Reveals decreasing undone tasks

Benefits of Checking Off Tasks:

- Visual progress

- Sense of accomplishment

- Motivation to continue

- Reduced stress

Feel the Satisfaction! Each checked task:

- Gives a sense of pride

- Encourages momentum

- Brings you closer to your goals

Keep Checking, Keep Moving! Regularly update your list to:

- Reflect completed tasks

- Adjust priorities

- Stay focused

Chapter Ten

Prioritize your tasks!

PRIORITIZE YOUR TASKS!

Urgent Tasks: A-List

- Complete same day

- High-priority tasks

- Deadlines today

Homework Priorities

- Check due dates

- Grade-dependent tasks

- A, B, or C-list depending on deadline

Task Categorization

- A-List (Today):

  - Urgent

  - High-priority

A list

1. Task
2. Task
3. Task
4. ...

- B-List (2-3 days):

  ○ Important

  ○ Medium-priority

- C-List (4-7 days):

  - Low-priority

  - Can wait

- D-List (Weekend):

  - Non-urgent

  - Extra chores

- X-List (Long-term):

  - "Nice to do"

  - Postponable

  - Special projects (e.g., trip planning)

Understand Your Lists

- A-List: Do today

- B-List: Do soon

- C-List: Do within a week

- D-List: Do on the weekend

- X-List: Do when time allows

Stay Organized

Review and update your lists regularly to:

- Ensure priorities are met

- Adjust task categories

- Stay focused

<table>
<tr><td>

A list

1. Task
2. Task
3. Task
4. ...

</td><td>

B list

1. Task
2. Task
3. Task
4. ...

</td></tr>
<tr><td>

C list

1. Task
2. Task
3. Task
4. ...

</td><td>

D list

1. Task
2. Task
3. Task
4. ...

</td><td>

X list

1. Task
2. Task
3. Task
4. ...

</td></tr>
</table>

Feeling Overwhelmed?

Don't worry!

Stay Calm, Stay Focused

- Long lists are manageable

- Break tasks into smaller steps

- Tackle one task at a time

Avoid Procrastination

- Don't put off critical tasks

- No task completes itself

- Schedule "spare time" as a task

Take Control

- Prioritize tasks

- Focus on one task

- Complete it

- Move to the next

Remember

- Every task counts

- Small steps lead to big progress

- Stay committed, stay successful!

Tips to Stay on Track

- Set timers for focused work

- Use breaks to recharge

- Review and adjust lists regularly

Chapter Eleven

Set Boundaries, Prioritize Time

LEARN TO SAY "NO!"

- Can't do everything in a day

- Prioritize tasks

- Protect your time

It's Okay to Say No

- To yourself: "Not now, later"

- To others: "I'm busy, sorry"

Why Saying No is Important

- Avoids overcommitting

- Reduces stress

- Preserves energy

- Maintains focus

Assertive Responses

- "I'm on a deadline, can't help now"

- "My plate is full, maybe later"

- "I need to prioritize my tasks"

Remember

- Saying no doesn't mean you're unhelpful

- It means you value your time and priori-ties

Practice Saying No

- Start small

- Be firm but polite

Effective Time Management Tips

Ask for More Time When Needed

- Overwhelmed with A-list tasks?

- Request an extension

- Demonstrate self-awareness and responsibility

Keep Promises, Build Trust

- Commit to a new deadline

- Follow through on your word

- Maintain credibility and reliability

Know Your Limits

- Understand your capabilities

- Assess task requirements

- Request help or adjustments when necessary

Self-Assessment is Key

- Recognize your strengths and weaknesses

- Evaluate task complexity

- Estimate required time accurately

Benefits of Honest Time Management

- Builds trust with others

- Reduces stress and pressure

- Fosters accountability

- Enhances self-awareness

Communicate Effectively

- "I need more time to complete this task"

- "I'll finish it by [new deadline]"

- "I'm not sure I can meet the deadline; can we discuss options?"

Remember

Honest time management = credibility and respect

Chapter Twelve

Develop Good Habits for Success

ORGANIZE YOUR SCHOOL ZONE

- Designate a specific area for school supplies

- Keep books, pencils, notes, and materials organized

- Easy access saves time and reduces stress

Study Smarter, Not Harder

* Use breaks to recharge

* Efficient study sessions:

  ◦ 30 minutes (younger students)

  ◦ 45-60 minutes (older students)

* Breaks help retain information and maintain focus

Benefits of Good Study Habits

* Improved concentration

* Better retention

* Reduced stress

* Increased productivity

Additional Tips

- Create a routine

- Set goals for each study session

- Review and adjust habits regularly

Study Break Ideas

- Take a short walk

- Stretch or exercise

- Grab a healthy snack

- Chat with a family member

Remember

- Good habits lead to academic success

- Stay organized, focused, and productive

Chapter Thirteen

Summary

FUEL YOUR BRAIN WITH Healthy Snacks!

What are they?

- Fresh fruits: apples, bananas, grapes

- Whole grain sandwiches

- Milk and 100% fruit juice (orange, apple)

Remember if you have allergies, then do not have anything that you are allergic to!

Minimize Distractions

- Turn off the TV and radio

- Find a quiet study space

- Focus on your tasks

Don't Forget Physical Activity!

- Exercise and play daily (at least 1 hour)

- Boosts energy and concentration

- Supports overall health and well-being

Benefits of Balance

- Improved focus and productivity

- Enhanced mental clarity

- Better physical health

- Increased motivation

Daily Routine Tips

- Schedule study time

- Set aside time for exercise and play

- Prioritize sleep (8-10 hours)

Remember

- *A healthy body and mind = academic success*

- Balance study time with physical activity!